MW01659782

Ten Essential Vocabulary Strategies

Practice for Success on Standardized Tests

Book 3

Lee Mountain

Educators Publishing Service
Cambridge and Toronto

Illustrations: © 1996-2004 JupiterImages, a division of Jupitermedia Corporation
Acquisitions/Development: Sethany Rancier
Cover Design: Karen Lomigora
Typesetting: Sarah Rakitin
Editor: Mary Troeger
Managing Editor: Sheila Neylon

ISBN 0-8388-3022-6
Printed in U.S.A.

Contents

Becoming a Word Whiz: What's in It for Me?

Tests! For some students, tests are as easy as pie. For others, a test is a bitter pill. What's the difference? Vocabulary.

There are vocabulary questions on every test. You expect to meet them on reading tests. But aren't they there on all your content-area tests, too? Science tests ask you about special terms. Math tests have a lot of word problems. In social studies, vocabulary questions include names of people and places as well as other new words. You answer questions about words on all tests.

Therefore, you want to know how to handle all the different types of vocabulary questions. The way a question is asked can surprise you, if you are not prepared. The wording can confuse you, if the question is worded in a different way.

Maybe you'll come upon new formats when you read the items on this year's standardized tests. Many a student has been tripped up by a "new look" for a test question. You don't want that to happen to you. And it won't—if you get ready for the top ten types of vocabulary questions.

This book will help you get ready. After you learn how to handle each type of question, you will be prepared. Then you can make your best possible score on vocabulary, no matter how the test questions are designed and worded.

Unit 1

The TOP TEN

types of vocabulary test questions

There are many ways to design questions about words. On tests, each question usually leads to four multiple-choice answers. But the questions vary in pattern and approach.

Here are ten types of vocabulary questions that are used on tests:

1. Meaning in sentence and passage
2. Context clues
3. Best words for blanks
4. Multiple meanings
5. Dictionary information
6. Figurative language
7. Synonyms and antonyms
8. Affixes and roots
9. Word relationships
10. Pairings

If you know how to handle each of these ten types of vocabulary questions, you will do well on tests.

A smart test taker reads a question about a word and then rereads the sentence in which the word appears. Rereading helps you focus on the word in context, that is, the words around it that determine its meaning. Sometimes you need to reread not just one sentence, but the whole paragraph. You will use context on almost all test questions about words. But you need a different approach for each of the top ten types of questions.

Let's look at the types, one by one. First, you'll see an example of each, with the answer explained in the "Think Aloud" section. Then you'll do "Practice for Success" exercises on test questions of that type. To conclude each lesson, there is an "Explain the Strategy" section, in which you will tell in your own words how you approach that type of vocabulary question.

Question type 1

Meaning in Sentence and Passage

Say the word *read* aloud. Does it sound like *reed* or *red*? You'll know in a flash each time you meet the word in a sentence. Look at this one: "Juan will *read* the book that his brother *read* last year." The first *read* sounds like *reed*, doesn't it? You know that the second *read* sounds like *red*, since "last year" makes it past tense.

On tests most of your vocabulary questions are about words in sentences and paragraphs. Often you can figure out a new word from the words around it. Try this question.

Example

What is the meaning of the word *secure* in this sentence?

She needed rope to secure the boat to the dock.

A. safe

B. drive

C. tie

D. steer

Think Aloud

The first answer, "A. safe," is tempting. You've heard people say, "Safe and secure." The words go together well. But the word *safe* would not fit in the sentence in place of *secure*. You could not say, "She needed rope to *safe* the boat to the dock." So you can reject the first answer. It can't be the right one.

The second answer, "B. drive," is a better fit, because *drive* is a verb, like the word *secure* in this sentence. But why would she need rope to *drive* the boat? You might ask the same question about the last answer, "D. steer." Why would she need rope to *steer* the boat? On a boat, rope is not used for *driving* or *steering*. Neither of those answers makes sense.

But it does make sense that she would need rope to *tie* the boat to the dock. The only answer that fits the sentence is "C. tie."

To practice, let's start with figuring out the meanings of words in sentences. Later, you will look at the whole paragraph. You can find context for a new word both within and beyond its sentence.

Practice for Success

Meaning in Sentence and Passage

1. What is the meaning of the word *appoints* in this sentence?
   The coach is in charge, so he appoints the captain of the team.

   A. praises

   B. plays

   C. chooses

   D. points at

2. What is the meaning of the word *occupied* in this sentence?
   After winning the election, the new prime minister and her staff occupied the offices in the government building.

   A. retreated from

   B. liked

   C. remodeled

   D. took over

3. What is the meaning of the word *obvious* in this sentence?
   The answers on the fourth-grade test seemed obvious to the seventh grader.

   A. clear

   B. written

   C. believable

   D. hard

4. What is the meaning of the word *contacts* in this paragraph?
Raphael will handle all contacts. All phone calls and e-mails will go through him. He will give you the names of people you should see. Ask him if you need help.

   A. connections

   B. lenses for eyes

   C. information

   D. letters

5. What is the meaning of the word *approbation* in this paragraph?
Lana was worthy of approbation. Her good deeds were known throughout the community. She had earned the support and approval of everyone.

   A. behavior

   B. praise

   C. goodness

   D. greetings

Explain the Strategy

Meaning in Sentence and Passage

Suppose you meet a new word on a test. How do the other words in its sentence or passage help you figure out the meaning of the new word?

____

____

____

Question type 2

Context Clues

Maybe you have never met the word *canine* before. But you can probably answer a context-clues question about *canine* if you look at the words around it for hints about its meaning.

Example

The performers in the canine show trotted onto the stage with much barking and tail-wagging.

Which words lead you to the meaning of *canine*?

A. *barking* and *tail-wagging*

B. *trotted* and *onto*

C. *show* and *much*

D. *performers* and *stage*

Think Aloud

As soon as you see the words *barking* and *tail-wagging,* you think about dogs, don't you? Those words are such strong context clues that they make the connection of the words *canine* and *dog* jump out at you. Perhaps you did not even bother to look at the other answers. Clearly the first answer is right. You know that a *canine* show has to be a *dog* show.

For some students, however, this type of question is confusing. They read the answers, looking for the word *dog*. Of course, it is not there. The question is, "Which words lead you to the meaning of *canine*?" It is <u>not</u> "What is the meaning of the word *canine*?"

This type of question asks you to find the words that make the meaning of a new word jump out at you. Those words are strong context clues, the kind you can't miss.

Now you will practice finding words that are strong context clues. You will also show that these context clues led you to the meaning of the new word.

Practice for Success

Context Clues

1. Joyce joined the school band because she liked playing tunes on her trumpet.
   Which words lead you to the meaning of the word *trumpet*?

   A. *Joyce* and *joined*

   B. *school* and *her*

   C. *band* and *tunes*

   D. *playing* and *because*

   Write a definition of the word *trumpet*. ______________________________

2. When Ned and Mike yelled angrily at each other, their teacher asked them to try to avoid that kind of conflict.
   Which words lead you to the meaning of the word *conflict*?

   A. *teacher* and *asked*

   B. *each* and *other*

   C. *avoid* and *when*

   D. *yelled* and *angrily*

   Write a definition of the word *conflict*. ______________________________

3. His moods are variable, with quick shifts from happy to sad.
   Which words lead you to the meaning of the word *variable*?

   A. *moods* and *sad*

   B. *happy* and *his*

   C. *quick* and *shifts*

   D. *from* and *are*

   Write a definition of the word *variable*. ______________________________

4. As she entered the twelve-story edifice, she found herself in a large carpeted lobby. Which words lead you to the meaning of *edifice*?

   A. *twelve-story* and *lobby*

   B. *entered* and *carpeted*

   C. *found* and *she*

   D. *herself* and *large*

   Write a definition of the word *edifice*. ________________________________

5. Though the berries were not ripe, they still looked edible, so he chewed a few of them. Which words lead you to the meaning of *edible*?

   A. *ripe* and *though*

   B. *still* and *so*

   C. *few* and *looked*

   D. *berries* and *chewed*

   Write a definition of the word *edible*. ________________________________

Explain the Strategy
Context Clues

Suppose you are asked to identify specific words that are context clues. What do you look for?

____

____

____

Question type 3

Best Words for Blanks

Choosing the best word for *one* blank is fairly easy. You reread the sentence several times, trying each answer in the blank. Then you choose the best fit. You've done that for years. But now your vocabulary tests may ask a harder type of question. They may ask you to choose the best words for *two* blanks. In this situation you need to look at the context of the sentence (or paragraph) to find any words that will give you help in deciding on the missing words.

Example

The team that wins the ____________ contest goes forward to play in the ____________ contest.

Which pair of words fits best in the two blanks?

A. *state* and *city*

B. *city* and *state*

C. *national* and *city*

D. *city* and *school*

Think Aloud

Before you try to choose the right answer, stop and think a minute about contests. If a team wins a small contest, what happens? It goes forward to play in a larger contest. Look for that "smaller/larger" relationship in the answers. Let's try each pair of words in the blanks.

First, answer A: "The team that wins the *state* contest goes forward to play in the *city* contest." Does that make sense? If your team won at the *state* level, would it then progress to the *city* level? No. That's not the way contests work. Winning teams move from competing in smaller areas to larger ones, as from school to city to state to national contests. It would be a step backward to move from state to city. So the first answer "A. *state* and *city*" would not make sense.

You run into the same trouble with the last two answers. But the second answer, "B. *city* and *state*" produces a very sensible sentence, with the *city* contest winners going forward to the *state* contest. That's the way contests work. So B is the correct answer.

Practice for Success
Best Words for Blanks

1. The chef served ____________ for the main course and ____________ for dessert.
   Which pair of words fits best in the two blanks?

   A. *spaghetti* and *stew*

   B. *ice cream* and *cake*

   C. *cookies* and *fish*

   D. *steak* and *pie*

2. The ____________ bee lays eggs, and the ____________ gather food.
   Which pair of words fits best in the two blanks?

   A. *queen* and *workers*

   B. *worker* and *drones*

   C. *drone* and *queens*

   D. *worker* and *queens*

3. All the ____________ in our solar system revolve around the ____________ .
   Which pair of words fits best in the two blanks?

   A. *stars* and *Earth*

   B. *planets* and *sun*

   C. *moons* and *stars*

   D. *planets* and *moons*

4. On the monitor of my __________, I see each word that I __________ on the keyboard.
   Which pair of words fits best in the two blanks?

   A. *screen* and *play*

   B. *computer* and *type*

   C. *television* and *find*

   D. *desk* and *draw*

5. Cindy was so __________ that her cousin seemed __________ in comparison.
   Which pair of words fits best in the two blanks?

   A. *fair* and *outgoing*

   B. *interesting* and *outgrown*

   C. *talkative* and *silent*

   D. *quiet* and *shy*

Explain the Strategy
Best Words for Blanks

Suppose you have to choose the best pair of words for two blanks. How do you approach that type of question?

____

____

____

Question type 4

Multiple Meanings

The word *ground* has many meanings. You might start by defining it as *soil* or *earth* or *foundation.* But many extended definitions spring from these basic meanings. Look at this list.

To break *ground* means to start digging on a building site.

To cover *ground* means to move a certain distance.

To get something off the *ground* means to get it started.

To build from the *ground* up means to do something thoroughly.

To run something into the *ground* means to overdo it.

A test question about *ground* will give you four answer choices. But each one of them might be a real definition of the word. Let's see how you can think your way through such a question.

Example

As Election Day approached, the candidate gained ground in the South.

Which meaning of *ground* fits the way it is used in the sentence above?

A. land

B. support

C. area

D. trail

Think Aloud

Reread the sentence. The word *gained* suggests that the candidate is making progress, perhaps rising in the polls. With this idea in mind, let's look at each answer.

The first answer is "A. land." Let's try it in the sentence: "As Election Day approached, the candidate gained *land* in the South." But it's not *land* that the candidate needs. It is *votes* from the people. So you reject the first answer and move to the second, "B. support."

"As Election Day approached, the candidate gained *support* in the South." Much better! Support from the voters is the kind of "ground" a candidate needs to gain.

A quick glance at the other two answers is all you need. You can reject "C. area" and "D. trail" for the same reasons as "A. land." In this sentence, the word *ground* means *support*.

Practice for Success
Multiple Meanings

1. She packed the suitcase lightly so as not to crush her cotton dress.
   Which meaning of the word *crush* fits best in the sentence above?

   A. press hard and break

   B. pound into bits

   C. conquer

   D. squeeze together tightly

2. The spark of a single firefly flickered in the darkness.
   Which meaning of the word *spark* fits best in the sentence above?

   A. small piece of burning matter

   B. flash of light

   C. bit of interest

   D. the jump of an electric current

3. After many hours of practice, the students gave a polished performance of their play.
   Which meaning of the word *polished* fits best in the sentence above?

   A. rubbed to a shine

   B. polite and refined

   C. improved and perfected

   D. bright

4. They needed a very tactful person to solve such a delicate problem.
Which meaning of the word *delicate* fits best in the sentence above?

A. light and soft

B. fine in quality

C. not strong

D. needing careful handling

5. The campers had a hard time of it, pitching their tents in the brush.
Which meaning of the word *brush* fits best in the sentence above?

A. land with a thick growth of small shrubs

B. light grazing stroke

C. equipment for painting

D. bushy tail, especially that of a fox

Explain the Strategy
Multiple Meanings

Suppose you are asked about a word that has four definitions. All four appear as answers. How do you choose the right one?

____

____

____

Question type 5

Dictionary Information Featuring Abbreviations

Some dictionary listings are half a page long. They go on and on, with definition after definition. How can you speed up finding the one you want? One way is to look at the abbreviations in the listing.

Dictionary abbreviations are not capitalized. You see n. for noun, v. for verb, and adj. for adjective. The other parts of speech have abbreviations too—adv. for adverb, conj. for conjunction, and pron. for pronoun. These abbreviations can help you speed to the right answer. Suppose this listing of the word *double* were given to you in a sample test question.

Example

double (dub´ ə) adj. 1. made for two. 2. twice as many.
n. 1. a look-alike. 2. a baseball hit that gets the batter to second base.
v. 1. to fold over. 2. to make twice as large.

Carolina is growing up to be a double of her mother.
Which dictionary definition fits the word *double* in the sentence above?

A. adj. 1

B. n. 1

C. n. 2

D. v. 2

Think Aloud

Most dictionary questions just ask you to pick the definition that fits. But you don't need to read *all* the definitions. In fact, you are wasting time if you do. Use the abbreviations. Read only the definitions for the right part of speech.

Look again at the sentence. "Carolina is growing up to be a double of her mother." See how the word *double* is used. What part of speech is it? It is a noun. So only the noun definitions are of any use to you. You can skip the adjective and verb definitions.

Since there is nothing about baseball in the sentence, you can reject n. 2. That leaves only n. 1, which defines a *double* as a look-alike. That fits. Answer B is correct.

Of course, some words are listed in the dictionary as only one part of speech. Then you will need to look at all the meanings. But for words with more than one part of speech, you can save time by skipping those that do not apply.

Practice for Success
Dictionary Information

Here is a paragraph in which you will read the word *right* many times. Below the paragraph is a dictionary listing of *right* and some questions about the word.

My math teacher wanted the *right* answers about *right* angles *right* away. But she said I had the *right* to ask for help. That's why I went *right* to her with my work. Then she could *right* any misunderstandings I had about the problems.

right (rīt) adj. 1. good. 2. proper. 3. accurate. n. 1. something to which a person has a fair claim. 2. the side opposite the left. adv. 1. completely. 2. directly. v. 1. to make correct. 2. to put in an upright position.

1. Which definition fits the use of *right* in the second sentence of the paragraph?
   A. adj. 1

   B. n. 1

   C. adv. 1

   D. v. 1

2. Which definition fits the use of *right* in the third sentence of the paragraph?
   A. adj. 2

   B. n. 2

   C. adv. 2

   D. v. 2

3. Which definition fits the use of *right* in the fourth sentence of the paragraph?
   A. adj. 3

   B. n. 1

   C. adv. 1

   D. v. 1

4. Look back at the first appearance of the word *right* in the first sentence of the paragraph. Which part of speech is it?

   A. adjective

   B. noun

   C. adverb

   D. verb

5. Read the definitions under the part of speech you chose in answer 4. Which fits best for the first appearance of the word *right*?
   A. the first definition

   B. the last definition

   C. neither of the above

   D. both of the above

Explain the Strategy
Dictionary Information

Suppose you are asked to find a dictionary definition that fits the way a word is used in a sentence. How can you speed up your hunt?

____

____

____

Question type 6

Figurative Language

In poetry, you expect to find figurative language, that is, language that extends the ordinary meaning of a word. But you come across it in prose, too. Can you recognize figurative language wherever and whenever you see it? You may have to show on a test that you really know the difference between figurative language and literal language.

Example

The words *over my head* appear in the four sentences below. In which sentence are the words used figuratively?

A. I pulled the covers over my head.

B. The balloon sailed high over my head.

C. The mistletoe was hanging over my head.

D. The last homework problem was over my head.

Think Aloud

The first three answers describe specific locations. They each use the literal meaning of the words. In answer A, the covers were really "over my head." In B, the balloon actually sailed "over my head." For C, the mistletoe was in fact hanging "over my head." These sentences mean exactly what they say.

But what about answer D: "The last homework problem was over my head." Is this sentence literal? Is the last homework problem floating in the air overhead? Hardly! When used figuratively, "over my head" means beyond my thinking, beyond my ability to figure out. So you would mark D as the answer in which "over my head" is used figuratively.

On tests you meet figurative language in many forms—similes, idioms, and other vivid expressions. The following exercises will show some of the approaches such questions can take.

Practice for Success
Figurative Language

1. At the height of six feet, five inches, the owner of the horse stood head and shoulders above the jockey. But he said the jockey was head and shoulders above him in horsemanship.

   The phrase "head and shoulders above" is used twice in the preceding paragraph. How would you describe the uses?

   A. both literal

   B. both figurative

   C. one literal and one figurative

   D. neither literal nor figurative

2. The curtain of night descended over the town.
   Which of the following sentences is a literal version of the preceding sentence?

   A. At nighttime the town became dark.

   B. People closed their curtains.

   C. Everyone turned on nightlights.

   D. Curtains descended all over town.

3. When Charlotte was awarded the medal, she looked ten feet tall.
   What do these words about Charlotte describe?

   A. her height

   B. her pride

   C. her prize

   D. her award

4. From the dark mountaintop, the line of cars wound downhill like a ribbon of light.
   At the end of the preceding sentence, what image does the simile convey?

   A. a ribbon on a road

   B. bright lights

   C. a ribbon unwinding from a spool

   D. a bright curving road

5. The screaming headlines made people stop and buy the newspaper.
What kind of headlines did you see in your mind's eye as you read the preceding sentence?

A. big, bold, black print

B. words shouted aloud

C. a newspaper buyer yelling

D. a newspaper stand with a loudspeaker

Explain the Strategy
Figurative Language

Suppose you are asked on a test about the difference between literal language and figurative language. How would you describe the difference?

____

____

____

Question type 7

Synonyms and Antonyms Featuring Comparison and Contrast

Often you may find two synonyms or two antonyms in the same sentence. One of them may help you figure out the meaning of the other. In addition, other words in the sentence (*but, rather than, however, like, as*) may signal a comparison that you can use. Look at the synonym question and the antonym question that follow.

Example

She was friendly and sociable, but her big brother was aloof.

What is a synonym of the word *sociable*?

A. able to be aloof

B. brotherly

C. friendly

D. society

What is an antonym of the word *aloof*?

A. older

B. sisterly

C. friendly

D. aloft

Think Aloud

Let's see if there is a comparison or a contrast in the test sentence. "She was friendly and sociable, but her big brother was aloof." The sister and brother are compared. Are they alike? No. The word *but* helps you know that they are different.

Now let's think about the possible synonyms in the sentence. Two words tell you about the sister. She is *friendly* and *sociable. Sociable* could be similar in meaning to *friendly* since the two words describe the same person. Maybe those two words are synonyms.

One word tells you about the brother. He is *aloof.* He is different from his friendly, sociable sister. He may be the very opposite of her. Maybe *aloof* is an antonym of *friendly*. Maybe it means *unfriendly*.

This train of thought leads you back to the answers. Have the comparison-contrast clues helped you? If so, you have arrived at the same letter for two correct answers: C. We have looked at only one sentence. But remember that the comparison-contrast clues might be throughout a paragraph. You may need to read more than one sentence as you look for clues.

Practice for Success

Synonyms and Antonyms

1. Breezes blew through the garden, carrying the scent of roses and the aroma of herbs.
   Which words in the sentence above are synonyms?

   A. *scent* and *aroma*

   B. *garden* and *roses*

   C. *blew* and *carrying*

   D. *herbs* and *through*

2. She dreaded leaving the cool library and walking home on the scorching streets.
   Which word in the sentence above is an antonym of *scorching*?

   A. leaving

   B. walking

   C. cool

   D. office

3. She wanted a permanent job rather than a temporary project.
   Which is the best synonym of *permanent* as the word is used in the sentence above?

   A. interesting

   B. lasting

   C. unchangeable

   D. ancient

4. Jim thought tennis was a safe sport. He saw no danger in playing baseball. Rock climbing, however, struck him as perilous.
   Which word in the paragraph above is an antonym of *perilous*?

   A. danger

   B. tennis

   C. sport

   D. safe

5. The talkativeness of a loquacious person can be wearing to a listener; the silence of a taciturn person is sometimes preferable.
Which pair of words from the preceding sentence are antonyms?

A. *talkativeness* and *silence*

B. *loquacious* and *taciturn*

C. both A. and B.

D. none of the above

Explain the Strategy

Synonyms and Antonyms

Suppose you meet a test question about synonyms or antonyms. How can comparison-contrast clues help you?

____

____

____

Question type 8

Affixes and Roots

Often you can determine the meaning of a compound word by putting its familiar parts together. Look at *earthquake, underwater, moonlight.* None of these words would give you trouble on a test. You can also handle short words that are clipped from longer words, such as *auto* from *automobile* and *fridge* from *refrigerator.*

But suppose you are asked about a word like *discontented.* That's harder. But you've learned that the prefix *dis* can mean *not.* You know that *contented* can mean *happy.* So you are able to put the parts together and say, "*Discontented* means *not happy.*"

For some vocabulary questions, however, you might not be able to piece together *all* the parts to construct the meaning. Maybe you can spot only *one* meaningful part. But that *one* familiar part can sometimes lead you to the answer.

Example

He set up his camera on a tripod.

What does the word *tripod* mean?

A. square table

B. rectangular base

C. platform with four legs

D. stand with three legs

Think Aloud

Let's think about the answers. A *tripod* has to be something that could hold a camera. But knowing that fact does not help you narrow down the answers. All four answers—a table, a base, a platform, or a stand—name things that could hold a camera. So the context is not leading you directly to the meaning of the word *tripod.*

But there is something familiar about the word *tripod,* something you have met before. There is a meaningful part at the beginning of the word *tripod. Tri* sounds familiar. You've heard it in the words *triangle* and *tricycle.* A triangle has *three* sides. A tricycle has *three* wheels. Maybe a *tripod* has *three* of something.

As soon as the *three* connection pops into your mind, you're on your way to the right answer. Only one of the choices mentions *three,* "D. stand with three legs." The familiar and meaningful prefix *tri* led you to the correct answer.

Practice for Success
Affixes and Roots

1. The driver glanced at the speedometer.
   What is the meaning of the word *speedometer*?

   A. instrument panel

   B. needle to show level of gas

   C. instrument to measure speed

   D. pedal to increase speed

2. Ms. Ruiz described telemarketing as a technique that many companies liked and most customers found annoying.
What is the meaning of the word *telemarketing*?

A. selling in stores

B. buying new editions

C. selling at a distance

D. buying close to home

3. The president will precede the secretary of state into the reception hall.
What is the meaning of the word *precede*?

A. go before

B. follow after

C. walk with

D. line up

4. There was a dent in the exhaust pipe.
What is the meaning of the word *exhaust*?

A. tube for incoming gas

B. entrance for air

C. opening for oil

D. place of outgoing fumes

5. The aquanauts performed experiments that produced valuable information.
What is the meaning of the word *aquanauts*?

A. space pioneers

B. scientists who work underwater

C. jewelers who sell turquoise stones

D. animals used in research

Explain the Strategy
Affixes and Roots

Suppose you are asked about a word with a meaningful part that you recognize. How can you use that part to help you figure out the meaning of the word?

____

____

____

Question type 9

Word Relationships Featuring Sound, Spelling, and Meaning

Words may be related in sound, spelling, or meaning. The words *I'll* and *aisle* sound the same, but they are spelled differently. Also, they have different meanings. Look at this sentence: The bride said, *"I'll* walk down the *aisle."*

Some words with the same spelling have two different meanings. Consider words like *deck* (ship or cards) and *crane* (bird or machine). Sometimes such words have different pronunciations. Look at *wind* (that blows your hat off) and *wind* (to coil thread around a spool). Even a few contractions have more than one meaning. *They'd* can mean *they had* or *they would.*

Jokes, wordplay, and riddles often play with these word relationships to give us a laugh. But, on a test, such words can be confusing. Look at this question.

Example

By agreeing to take turns using the computer, Bill and Sue avoided an angry row in class.

What is the meaning of the word *row* in the sentence above?

A. movement with oars

B. trip over water

C. items arranged in a line

D. quarrel

Think Aloud

Maybe your first thought about the word *row* is the rowboat connection. But there is something wrong with that picture. Reread the sentence. "By agreeing to take turns using the computer, Bill and Sue avoided an angry row in class." The context does not lead you toward answers that have anything to do with water. So the first two answers, "A. movement with oars" and "B. trip over water," don't seem to fit.

The third answer, "C. items arranged in a line" is a *maybe*. Maybe Bill and Sue were looking at a row of seats in the class. But the wording "avoided an angry row" does not make sense with the rest of the sentence.

This leads you to take a hard look at "D. quarrel." Though you may never before have connected the word *row* with the meaning *quarrel*, you have to think, "Maybe." The word *angry* goes well with *quarrel*. An "angry row" could be a quarrel.

If you know the word *rowdy* (noisy and quarrelsome), this might lead you to a different pronunciation of *row* (rhyming with *now*), giving more certainty to your choice. But if you don't know *rowdy*, "D. quarrel" still makes the best choice.

Trying to use "relationship thinking" can help you on a test, even with words that are brand new to you. It can also help you in your regular reading, whenever you have to figure out a strange word.

Practice for Success
Word Relationships

1. If she'd been more careful, she would not have cut her finger.
   In the sentence above, what is the meaning of *she'd*?

   A. shed

   B. she would

   C. she should

   D. she had

2. The farmer decided to sow wheat on all his land.
   In the sentence above, what is the meaning of the word *sow*?

   A. female hog

   B. plant

   C. sew

   D. therefore

3. He thought he couldn't play well, even though he often threw the ball through the hoop.
   In the sentence above, which word means "in one side and out the other"?

   A. through

   B. threw

   C. thought

   D. though

4. The horse tossed his mane as he paraded down Main Street with the mien of a leader.
   Which word from the sentence above means "bearing, manner of conducting oneself"?

   A. mane

   B. main

   C. mien

   D. none of the above

5. Which word means "a person who inherits money from a relative"?

A. hare

B. heir

C. ere

D. air

Explain the Strategy
Word Relationships

On a test, suppose you are asked about a word that has a special relationship with other words because of its sound, spelling, or meaning. How will you think your way through the question?

____

____

____

Question type 10

Pairings Featuring Text and Graphics

Have you ever searched for information about a topic on the Internet? Did you find and read only *one* Web site about it? Or did you find *more than one*? If your answer is *more than one*, you have already started reading what test makers call "paired passages." You have read about the same topic from more than one source.

On a test you may be asked to read material from different sources to answer questions. You might have a poem, a paragraph, and a picture used in combination. Test makers expect you to draw information from all the sources provided to answer the vocabulary questions.

In the example below, you will work with three sources of information—a picture, some prose, and several lines of poetry.

Example

A Vivid Image

Using its claws, the eagle perches proudly and securely on a spike of rock jutting up from a steep stony cliff. High above the ocean waters, he is surrounded by the blue sky. The poet Alfred, Lord Tennyson, summed up his image of the eagle in these lines.

He clasps the crag with crooked hands.
Close to the sun in lonely lands,
Ringed with the azure world, he stands.

Which word from the poem is defined in the paragraph?

A. crag

B. clasps

C. crooked

D. close

Think Aloud

When you reread the paragraph, you'll probably slow down as you come upon "a spike of rock jutting up from a steep stony cliff." That sounds like a definition. And it is. It's a definition of *crag*. You know from the poem that a *crag* is some type of perch. You know from the paragraph what type. The paragraph gives you some help with the other answers. But it helps you the most with the first answer, "A. crag."

You just put together the meaning of *crag* from more than one source. The poem used the word in context. The paragraph gave a definition. And the picture clarified the image. You used all the sources as you figured out the meaning of the new word.

Practice for Success

Pairings

1. Look back at the picture, paragraph, and poem about the eagle. They can help you figure out the meaning of the word *azure* in the poem. What does *azure* mean?

   A. above

   B. stone

   C. steep

   D. blue

2. You met the words "crooked hands" in the poem. What word from the paragraph could be a synonym for these words?

   A. perch

   B. claws

   C. poet

   D. image

3. Which word in the paragraph helps you understand the words "close to the sun" in the poem?

   A. jutting

   B. waters

   C. spikes

   D. high

4. The picture of the eagle is the graphic, or illustration, that goes with the paired passages. It helps you understand the words in ____________ .

   A. the paragraph

   B. the poem

   C. both A. and B.

   D. none of the above

5. From what source or sources do you learn the name of the poet who wrote about the eagle?

A. the paragraph

B. the poem

C. the picture

D. all of the above

Explain the Strategy

Pairings

Suppose you meet a test question about pairings of text and graphics. How do you handle that type of question?

____

____

____

Unit 2

Practice TEST PASSAGES

with vocabulary questions

Test passages come from many different kinds of writing—fiction and nonfiction, poetry and prose. You will answer vocabulary questions about them. Here are the kinds of writing you will see in the practice tests for this book.

1. Fiction
2. Biography
3. Informational article
4. Fable
5. Classic
6. Letter
7. Content-area material
8. Beliefs
9. Wordplay
10. Pairings

Again and again in these practice tests, you will meet the top ten types of vocabulary questions. Following each question is the name and number of its type. Sometimes two types (or strategies) are equally helpful in figuring out an answer. In these cases, two numbers are given.

If you have trouble with a question, turn back to its pages in Unit 1. Reread and review the strategy for approaching that type of question. Then try again. You will probably be able to figure out the correct answer.

Five multiple-choice questions and a bonus question follow each practice test passage. Working with the different kinds of questions about varied reading selections will help your vocabulary develop and grow.

1. Fiction: BLUE JAY TALK
adapted from *A Tramp Abroad* by Mark Twain

Animals talk to each other, of course. There can be no question about that. But I suppose 1
there are very few people who can understand them. I never knew but one man who could. I knew he could, however, because he told me so himself.

He was a miner who had lived in a lonely corner of California among the woods and moun- 2
tains a good many years. He'd studied the ways of his only neighbors, the beasts and the birds, until he believed he could understand any remark they made.

This was Jim Baker. According to Jim Baker, some animals have only a limited education and 3
use only very simple words and scarcely ever a metaphor to make a lively comparison. But other animals have a large vocabulary and a fine command of language. These latter talk a great deal. They like it. They are conscious of their talent, and they enjoy showing off.

Baker said that blue jays were the best talkers he had found among birds and beasts. He had 4
heard them jawing and disputing and sounding off with as many leather-headed opinions as a crowd of humans. Said he: "Whatever a blue jay feels, he can put into language. And no mere commonplace language, either, but rattling, out-and-out book-talk! Bristling with metaphor, too—just bristling! And as for command of language, why you never see a blue jay get stuck for a word. Nobody ever did. Words just boil out of him."

Vocabulary Questions

1. Which meaning of *remark* fits the way the word is used in paragraph 2?

   A. a comment

   B. mark again

   C. notice

   D. observe

Question type (1) **:Meaning in Sentence and Passage** *and*

Question type (4) **:Multiple Meanings**

2. In paragraph 2, what is the meaning of the underlined word *he'd*?

   A. heed

   B. he would

   C. he had

   D. head

Question type (9) **:Word Relationships**

3. In paragraph 3, Mark Twain mentions the use of metaphor. Jim Baker says in paragraph 4 that blue jay language is "bristling with metaphor." Which of these words from paragraphs 3 and 4 do the best job of describing *metaphor*?

   A. limited education

   B. lively comparison

   C. conscious of their talent

   D. commonplace language

Question type (2) :**Context Clues**

4. Which of these expressions from paragraph 4 are vivid wordings?

   A. rattling, out-and-out book-talk

   B. jawing and sounding off

   C. leather-headed opinions

   D. all of the above

Question type (6) :**Figurative Language**

5. Which synonym of *disputing* best fits the way the word is used in paragraph 4?

   A. fist-fighting

   B. arguing loudly

   C. debating calmly

   D. denying

Question type (1) :**Meaning in Sentence and Passage** *and*
Question type (7) :**Synonyms and Antonyms**

BONUS Question: According to this passage, what can a metaphor do? (See paragraph 3.)

____

____

2. Biography: ARGENTINA'S EVITA

North America has come to know, by nickname, a great lady of South America. Her nick- 1
name has been used as the title of a Broadway musical and a movie. Evita! Her full name was
Maria Eva Duarte Peron. But she was always better known as Evita. Even when she was the
first lady of Argentina, she did not become pretentious. She was so down-to-earth that she
wanted everyone to call her by her nickname.

Born in poverty in 1919, Evita moved from her small ____________ to the big ____________ 2
of Buenos Aires. There she became an actress. At a concert to help the survivors of an earth-
quake, she met her future husband, Juan Peron. Both of them worked hard to help the poor.

When Peron ran for president of Argentina, Evita helped him win. Together they tried to tackle 3
the health problems of the country. Evita started programs to control diseases. She also per-
suaded her husband to give women the right to vote.

At the height of her power, her health failed. Evita had cancer. Week after week, she was in 4
severe and unceasing pain. But she still wanted to join her husband in the motorcade the
week of his second election. Sadly, when the time came, she was too weak to stand up in the
car. So Evita had herself propped up on a metal support that she hid with a bulky fur coat.
She waved to the people she loved one last time.

Death claimed Eva Peron in 1952. Her name lives on in music, however. She is well remem- 5
bered on stage and screen as Evita.

Vocabulary Questions

1. In paragraph 1, which pair of words are antonyms?

   A. *musical* and *movie*

   B. *Eva* and *Evita*

   C. *first lady* and *nickname*

   D. *down-to-earth* and *pretentious*

Question type (7) **:Synonyms and Antonyms**

2. Which are the best words for the blanks in paragraph 2?

   A. *country* and *street*

   B. *village* and *city*

   C. *house* and *room*

   D. *town* and *farm*

Question type (3) **:Best Words for Blanks**

3. Here is a dictionary listing of the word *tackle*.

tackle (tak'əl) n. 1. fishing equipment. 2. football player next to either end. v. 1. undertake to solve. 2. seize.

Which definition fits the way the underlined word *tackle* is used in paragraph 3?

A. the first noun definition

B. the second noun definition

C. the first verb definition

D. the second verb definition

Question type (5) **:Dictionary Information**

4. In paragraph 4, what is the meaning of the underlined word *unceasing*?

A. not stopping

B. hurtful

C. unhappy

D. off and on

Question type (8) **:Affixes and Roots**

5. Which words in paragraph 4 are the context clues that make the meaning of *support* clear to you?

A. *propped* and *metal*

B. *fur* and *coat*

C. *herself* and *Evita*

D. *height* and *power*

Question type (2) **:Context Clues**

BONUS Question: What was Eva Peron's *sobriquet*? (Use your dictionary to find the meaning of this unusual word.)

____

3. Informational Article: ELIZABETH COCHRANE: AN INVESTIGATIVE REPORTER

Today on television you often see and hear stories from investigative reporters. The stories 1
usually tell the public important information that has been kept secret. To uncover the facts, reporters may work in surprising ways. They may pretend to apply for a job at a business that they want to look at from the inside. When they interview people, they may not say they are working on a story.

Reporters of long ago used these methods, too. One of the first female reporters to write 2
important investigative stories was Elizabeth Cochrane. She lived from 1867 to 1922.

In those days, it was hard for a woman to get a job as a reporter. Elizabeth had managed to 3
find work in Pittsburgh. But when she moved to New York, she could not find a job. It was months before she got a break.

The editor of the *New York World* newspaper wanted a story about a mental hospital. He 4
hoped to get an *inside* report of what was going on there. This editor asked Elizabeth if she thought she could get herself admitted as a mental patient. Elizabeth knew she might be turned away from the hospital. But she had pretended before, to get a story. She thought she could do it again. And she succeeded! After ten days inside the hospital, Elizabeth was ready to write. She had earned her new job.

One of the greatest rewards for a reporter is making a difference. Elizabeth Cochrane's story 5
about the hospital made a difference. People were outraged when they read how patients were treated. They demanded change. So, because of the work of this ______________ reporter, the hospital was compelled to ______________.

Vocabulary Questions

1. Which of these words from paragraph 1 are the context clues that make the meaning of *investigative* clear to you?

   A. *reporters* and *public*

   B. *facts* and *ways*

   C. *interview* and *business*

   D. *secret* and *uncover*

Question type (2): **Context Clues**

2. You read the words *long ago* in paragraph 2. In this passage what do those words mean?

A. about fifty years ago

B. about a hundred years ago

C. about one hundred fifty years ago

D. about two hundred years ago

Question type (1) **:Meaning in Sentence and Passage**

3. In paragraph 3, what does the underlined word *break* mean?

A. smash

B. chance

C. fracture

D. brake

Question type (1) **:Meaning in Sentence and Passage**

4. Which meaning of *admitted* fits the way the word is used in paragraph 4?

A. confessed

B. granted

C. let in

D. allowed

Question type (4) **:Multiple Meanings**

5. In paragraph 5, what is the best pair of words for the two blanks?

A. *investigative* and *improve*

B. *female* and *open*

C. *young* and *reply*

D. *hard-working* and *report*

Question type (3) **:Best Words for Blanks**

BONUS Question: In Elizabeth Cochrane's chosen career, why would she need an extensive vocabulary?

____

____

____

4. Fable: THE WOLF IN SHEEP'S CLOTHING

One morning a hungry wolf woke up in his lair, trotted outside, and discovered the skin of a 1
large sheep on the ground. It was wooly and soft and white. As he looked at it, he thought of a plan.

"If I put this on," he said to himself, "I will look just like a sheep. I will be able to enter the 2
pasture nearby without the lambs knowing that I am a wolf. If one of them strays to the edge of the field, I can easily carry the little creature to my den for dinner." The wolf licked his lips at the thought.

He threw the big woolly sheepskin over his head and back. It covered him well. He slipped in 3
easily among the sheep and lambs. Near the gate, the wolf ______________ one little lamb who had ______________ away from the flock. He crept toward the lamb.

Before he could spring upon it, however, the shepherd walked through the gate and closed it 4
behind him. The wolf stood as still as a stone statue. "I need a big fat sheep for my meal," he muttered, looking around. "Let me see. Which one shall it be?" Before the wolf could move, the shepherd chose him. And that was the end of the wolf in sheep's clothing.

It is unwise to pretend to be something you are not. 5

Vocabulary Questions

1. Sometimes a person is called "a wolf in sheep's clothing." What does this metaphor mean?

    A. someone who puts on a false front

    B. a person who eats very fast

    C. a person who tames animals

    D. somebody who wears woolen clothes

Question type 6 **:Figurative Language**

2. What group of words in paragraph 1 gives you a strong context clue about the meaning of *lair*?

   A. one morning

   B. discovered the skin

   C. a large sheep

   D. woke up in

Question type (2) **:Context Clues**

3. In paragraph 3, which two words are best for the blanks?

   A. *saw* and *marched*

   B. *called* and *galloped*

   C. *spotted* and *wandered*

   D. *devoured* and *walked*

Question type (3) **:Best Words for Blanks**

4. Which meaning of *spring* best fits the way the word is used in paragraph 4?

   A. season after winter

   B. jump

   C. open or close quickly

   D. underground source of water

Question type (4) **:Multiple Meanings**

5. In paragraph 5 what is the meaning of the underlined word *unwise*?

   A. ill-advised

   B. not sensible

   C. imprudent

   D. all of the above

Question type (8) **:Affixes and Roots**

BONUS Question: What is the maxim of this fable? (Use your dictionary if you are not sure of the meaning of this word.)

____

____

5. Classic: GULLIVER IN THE LAND OF THE GIANTS adapted from *Gulliver's Travels* by Jonathan Swift

Introduction:
Time and again, Gulliver was shipwrecked in strange lands. His best-known adventure was in the land of the tiny people. But he also had adventures in the land of the giants. Here is what happened his first day in that land.

Walking <u>inland</u> from the beach, I soon found myself in a field of corn that grew at least forty 1
feet high. Then I heard a noise in the air, like thunder. I saw a huge foot coming toward me. Again that noise—followed by the rushing sound of falling stalks of corn! Then I knew that a giant of a man was cutting the corn nearby, and I was soon to be buried under it. I screamed as loud as fear could make me.

The huge farmer stood motionless. Then he bent down and spotted me. He reached out care- 2
fully, as if he were going to touch a small but deadly creature that might bite or sting him. Finally, he picked me up between his thumb and forefinger and held me about three yards from his eyes.

There I hung, more than sixty feet from the ground, pinched most painfully in his grasp. I 3
groaned loudly. That seemed to let him know how much the pressure of his thumb and finger hurt me. Gently he put me back on the ground on all fours, and he knelt to watch me. At once I got to my feet and made a low <u>bow</u> to him.

Taking out his handkerchief, he spread it on his open hand, which he placed flat on the 4
ground. He motioned for me to step up on it. I did and he carried me ______________ to his house.

Vocabulary Questions

1. In the introduction, which word is the context clue that tells you Gulliver traveled by water?

   A. adventure

   B. land

   C. people

   D. shipwrecked

Question type (2) **:Context Clues**

2. In paragraph 1, what is the meaning of the underlined word *inland*?

   A. island

   B. toward the water

   C. away from the water

   D. in the water

Question type (8) **:Affixes and Roots**

3. In paragraph 2, one sentence contains a comparison that helps you know the farmer's feelings about Gulliver. Which sentence?

   A. first

   B. second

   C. third

   D. fourth

Question type (6) **:Figurative Language**

4. In paragraph 3, what is the meaning of the underlined word *bow*?

   A. a bending of the body in greeting

   B. a curve

   C. device for shooting arrows

   D. stick for playing the violin

Question type (4) **:Multiple Meanings** *and*

Question type (9) **:Word Relationships**

5. In paragraph 4, what is the best word for the blank?

A. strayed

B. strait

C. straight

D. strained

Question type (3) **:Best Words for Blanks** *and*

Question type (9) **:Word Relationships**

BONUS Question: The book *Gulliver's Travels* is called a classic. What is a *classic*? (Use your dictionary if you are not sure.)

____

____

____

6. Letter: TO HARRIET TUBMAN, PRAISING HER HEROISM from FREDERICK DOUGLASS

During her life Harriet Tubman's name was not as well known as it is today. She had to do much of her work in secret. She helped slaves flee to northern states and to Canada where they could be free. All along her route, people were willing to help. Some hid the slaves and gave them food. Others carried them part of the way north. Harriet Tubman's helpers bore witness to their belief in freedom for everyone. 1

Frederick Douglass, who fought publicly to free the slaves, wrote to Harriet Tubman in 1868. He wanted her to know how much he admired her work. This is part of his letter. 2

"The difference between us is very marked. Most that I have done and suffered in the service of our cause has been in public. I have received much encouragement every step of the way. You, on the other hand, have labored in a private way. 3

"I have labored in the day—you in the night. I have had the applause of the crowd and the satisfaction that comes from being approved by the multitude. Most of what you have done has been witnessed by a few trembling, scarred, and footsore men and women whom you have led out of the house of bondage. Their heartfelt 'God bless you' has been your only reward. The midnight sky and the silent stars have been the witnesses of your ______________ to freedom and of your heroism." 4

Vocabulary Questions

1. Which pairs of antonyms from Douglass's letter show the difference between Frederick Douglass and Harriet Tubman?

    A. *public* and *private*

    B. *day* and *night*

    C. *multitude* and *few*

    D. all of the above

Question type (7) **:Synonyms and Antonyms**

2. The word *witness* is used in paragraph 1 and forms of the word appear twice in paragraph 4. Which meaning of *witness* applies to paragraph 4?

    A. to see, to be present at

    B. to express openly

    C. to offer written proof

    D. to tell in court

Question type (4) **:Multiple Meanings** *and*

Question type (10) **:Pairings**

3. Which meaning of *cause* matches the way the word is used in paragraph 3?

    A. something that brings about an effect

    B. whatever leads to a result

    C. a movement that people support

    D. reason

Question type (4) **:Multiple Meanings**

4. Who were the "trembling, scarred, and footsore men and women" that Douglass wrote about in paragraph 4?

    A. Tubman's helpers

    B. Douglass's helpers

    C. people who had escaped to Canada

    D. slaves who were fleeing

Question type (1) **:Meaning in Sentence and Passage**

5. In paragraph 4, what word do you think Fredrick Douglass used in the blank?

   A. attention

   B. devotion

   C. chase

   D. light

Question type (3) **:Best Words for Blanks**

BONUS Question: Reread the quotation from Fredrick Douglass's letter. Many letters of today are sent by e-mail. What are the differences in style and vocabulary between his letter and an e-mail letter?

____

____

____

7. Content-Area Material: SAFETY IN SCIENCE LABORATORIES

Laboratories range from simple to elaborate. Science labs for beginners may have only basic equipment for conducting easy experiments. Laboratories for advanced students may be equipped with lots of complex apparatus. In all labs, however, safety is a major concern. 1

Often safety features are literally "built in." Builders provide ventilating hoods above lab tables. Fans inside these hoods draw up fumes so that the air in the lab will not be polluted. Sinks, built into laboratory tables, allow for quick cleaning of test tubes, beakers, and flasks after use. Safety rules are posted for all to see. Fire alarm systems and fire extinguishers provide further protection against accidents. 2

Safety experts recommend protective clothing and safety goggles for experiments with hazardous substances. But the best safeguard of all against laboratory accidents is a person who always thinks about safety. 3

Vocabulary Questions

1. In paragraph 1 which pair of words are antonyms?

   A. *complex* and *elaborate*

   B. *safety* and *concern*

   C. *elaborate* and *simple*

   D. *range* and *conducting*

Question type (7) **:Synonyms and Antonyms**

2. What synonym of *apparatus* in paragraph 1 gives you the meaning of the word?

A. equipment

B. laboratory

C. basic

D. advanced

Question type 7 **:Synonyms and Antonyms**

3. Here are four dictionary definitions of **ventilate** (ven′ tə lāt) v. 1. to bring fresh air into a room. 2. to draw gases out of a room. 3. to discuss feelings openly. 4. to provide oxygen.

Which definition describes the action of the ventilating hoods mentioned in paragraph 2?

A. 1

B. 2

C. 3

D. 4

Question type 5 **:Dictionary Information**

4. Circle the piece of lab equipment that is NOT mentioned in paragraph 2.

A. 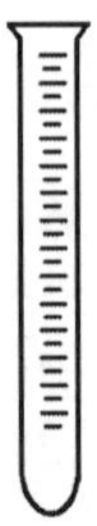

B. 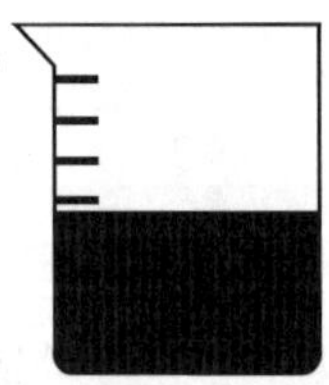

C. 

D. 

Question type 10 **:Pairings**

5. The suffix *ous* appears at the end of many words, such as *dangerous*, *perilous*, and (in paragraph 3) *hazardous*. What meaning does *ous* convey?

A. best

B. better

C. full of

D. one who

Question type 8 **:Affixes and Roots**

BONUS Question: Write a safety rule that you think would be important in a science laboratory.

____

____

8. Beliefs: ABOUT GREATNESS

In his play, *Twelfth Night,* Williams Shakespeare wrote:
Some are born great,
some achieve greatness,
and some have greatness thrust upon them.

In his poem, "A Psalm of Life," Henry Wadsworth Longfellow wrote:
Lives of great men all remind us
We can make our lives sublime
And, departing, leave behind us
Footprints on the sands of time.

Vocabulary Questions

1. In which category would Shakespeare place a vice president who, because of the death of the president, suddenly had to lead the country in a time of crisis?

   A. born great

   B. achieved greatness

   C. had greatness thrust upon him

   D. all of the above

Question type (1) **:Meaning in Sentence and Passage**

2. What synonym of the word *great* do you find in Longfellow's lines?

   A. lives

   B. remind

   C. departing

   D. sublime

Question type (7) **:Synonyms and Antonyms**

3. Where do you find a figurative image of greatness?

A. in Shakespeare's lines

B. in Longfellow's lines

C. in both of the above

D. in neither of the above

Question type (6) **:Figurative Language** *and*
Question type (10) **:Pairings**

4. Here is a dictionary listing of the word *thrust*.

thrust (thrust) v. 1. to push with sudden force. 2. to pierce or stab. n. 1. forward movement. 2. energy or drive.

Which definition gives the meaning of Shakespeare's use of *thrust*?

A. the first verb definition

B. the second verb definition

C. the first noun definition

D. the second noun definition

Question type (5) **:Dictionary Information**

5. Longfellow wrote, "*We* can make our lives sublime." According to Shakespeare's categories, in which group do *We* belong?

A. born great

B. achieve greatness

C. have greatness thrust upon

D. all of the above

Question type (10) **:Pairings**

BONUS Question: What words would you use to describe a great person?

___

___

___

9. Wordplay: THE FORTUNE INSIDE THE COOKIE

Do you think fortune cookies are baked in the kitchen of each Chinese restaurant? Do you 1
think the baker carefully puts the strip of paper with a fortune on it inside each cookie? If so, think again. Today, very few fortune cookies are specially prepared at the restaurant. Instead they are mixed, baked, and wrapped by the thousands in factories.

The process starts with truckloads of sugar and flour. These basic items are dumped into a 2
steel vat with water, soybean oil, yellow dye, and other ingredients. After the batter is mixed, it is pumped out in little circles, like pancakes. While these circles are still hot from the ovens, the little strips of paper carrying fortunes drop in the center. Then each cookie is pressed into a mold to get its special shape. The last step is wrapping.

Fortune cookies are crunchy and sweet. You may like their taste. But the thing that sets them 3
apart from other cookies is the strip of paper inside. You pull it out as soon as you break the cookie because it is fun to read ________________ fortune. Maybe you compare fortunes with the other people at your table. The fortunes are written so that they usually bring grins rather than grimaces. Look at these samples.

Your charm exceeds that of the trinket on your bracelet.

If you are as spineless as a marionette, someone else will work your strings.

A clinging vine is more attractive as a plant than as a person.

Vocabulary Questions

1. In paragraph 2, what is the meaning of the underlined word *vat*?

   A. large container

   B. cookie sheet

   C. kettle

   D. hot stove

Question type (1) **:Meaning in Sentence and Passage**

2. Which of these words from paragraph 2 is not a compound word?

   A. truckloads

   B. soybean

   C. pancakes

   D. fortune

Question type (8) **:Affixes and Roots**

3. Read these definitions of the word *mold*.

mold (mōld) n. 1. a form for shaping. 2. a pattern. v. 1. to fit closely. 2. to influence strongly.

Which definition best fits the way the underlined word *mold* is used in paragraph 2?

A. the first noun definition

B. the second noun definition

C. the first verb definition

D. the second verb definition

Question type (5) **:Dictionary Information**

4. Read the sample fortunes on the strips of paper. Which word or words have a double meaning?

A. charm

B. strings

C. clinging vine

D. all of the above

Question type (9) **:Word Relationships**

5. In paragraph 3, what is the best word for the blank?

A. *you're*

B. *your*

C. *its*

D. all of the above

Question type (3) **:Best Words for Blanks** *and*

Question type (9) **:Word Relationships**

BONUS Question: The fortunes on fortune-cookie strips are meant to "bring grins rather than grimaces." What is a *grimace*? (Use your dictionary if you don't know this word.)

____

____

10. Pairings: RELATED PROSE, POETRY, AND GRAPHIC ABOUT THE STATUE OF LIBERTY

The lines below are from the poem "The New Colossus" by Emma Lazarus (1849–1887). They 1
appear on the base of the Statue of Liberty, which stands in New York harbor. In only thirty-six words, they welcomed all newcomers. They gave encouragement to people who were beginning a new life.

For many years, Lady Liberty, as she is also known, was the first sight many immigrants had 2
of this country. Those who arrived in the 1800s often came from crowded cities where work was hard to find. Some were trying to escape from countries with unjust leaders. Others hoped to find land to farm.

Many voyaged across the Atlantic Ocean to get to the United States. They endured storms that 3
built to the strength of tempests. Once here, they often had little money, and few belongings, but great dreams for a better life. For them, Lady Liberty's torch was the light of hope.

Lines from "The New Colossus" 4
Give me your tired, your poor,
Your huddled masses yearning to breathe free,
The wretched refuse of your teeming shore.
Send these, the homeless tempest-tossed to me.
I lift my lamp beside the golden door.

Vocabulary Questions

1. Which meaning fits the parts of the underlined word *newcomers* as it is used in paragraph 1?

   A. recent arrivals

   B. first ships

   C. more people

   D. fresh movers

Question type (8) **:Affixes and Roots**

2. In the poem, which words refer to the people who came to our country in the 1800s?

   A. golden door

   B. teeming shore

   C. tired, poor

   D. breathe free

Question type (2) **:Context Clues**

3. What is the meaning of the word *tempest* in the poem and in paragraph 3 of the article?

   A. rain shower

   B. storm on the ocean

   C. storm on land

   D. tornado

Question type (10) **:Pairings**

4. The picture shows Lady Liberty holding something. Which words in the paragraphs and in the poem name what it is?

   A. *money* and *dreams*

   B. *people* and *life*

   C. *masses* and *homeless*

   D. *torch* and *lamp*

Question type (10) **:Pairings**

5. What does the underlined word *golden* mean as it is used in the last line of the poem?

   A. made of gold

   B. covered with gold

   C. hopeful or better

   D. shining

Question type (6) **:Figurative Language**

BONUS Question: The lines on the Statue of Liberty are from a poem entitled "The New Colossus." What is a *colossus*? (Use your dictionary if you don't know the meaning of this word.)

____

____

Unit 3

MORE PRACTICE on

vocabulary through wordplay

Wordplay is a great way to extend your vocabulary. Let's revisit some of the word work you did in the first two units by solving a few puzzles and riddles.

Here are several ways to play with synonyms, figurative language, spelling and meaning connections, and other topics related to the top ten types of vocabulary questions. Building your vocabulary through wordplay can also be fun.

1. Cross-Synonym Puzzles
2. Mix-Matching Meaningful Parts
3. Animal Metaphors
4. Coloring the Meaning
5. Clipping Words
6. Riddle Pairs

1. Cross-Synonym Puzzles

```
    T
    E
    R
    R
HORRIBLE
    B
    L
    E
```

A cross-synonym puzzle starts with a pair of synonyms. Let's use the synonyms *terrible* and *horrible.* Print *terrible* vertically. Then print *horrible* horizontally where the letters cross.

```
    T
    E
 ALARMING
    R
HORRIBLE
    B
AWFUL
    E
```

Your challenge is to think of synonyms of *terrible* and *horrible* that have a common letter with one of the two crossed words. If you came up with *awful* and *alarming,* you can add them to the cross-synonym puzzle.

Another person might add the word *fearful* rather than *awful.* That's fine. It fits. Someone also might add the word *tough* horizontally at the top since it can be a synonym of *terrible.* If there is room, you can also add synonyms vertically. You could start down from the F in *awful* and add *frightening.*

Now think of a pair of synonyms to start a cross-synonym puzzle of your own. Print them vertically and horizontally in the following grid. Long words like *attractive* and *handsome* are good choices because they give you room to add other synonyms. Include at least five synonyms in your cross-synonym puzzle. As you search for synonyms, the thesaurus is your best friend.

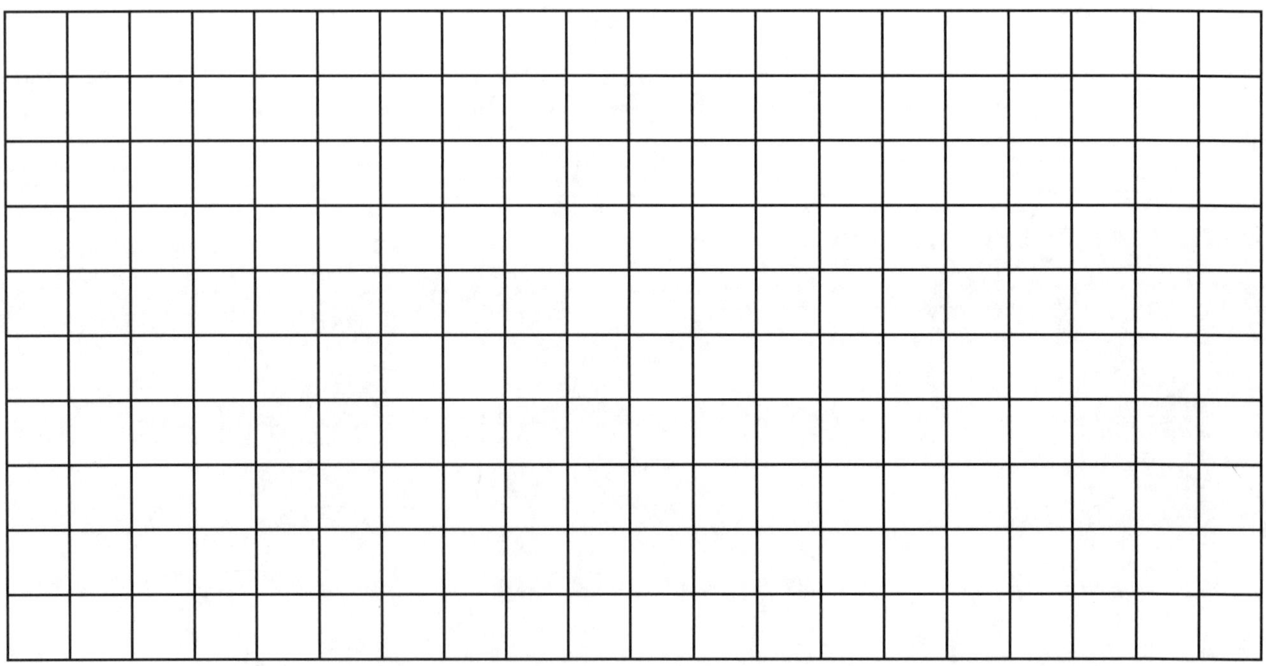

2. Mix-Matching Meaningful Parts

With three beginnings and three endings, how many words do you think you can build? ______

Beginnings	Endings
re	quest
in	form
con	fer

On your first look at the beginnings and endings, you might read across and see three words. List them. Then use each in a sentence.

1. ______

2. ______

3. ______

Now start mix-matching. You can put together six other words. List them. Use each one in a sentence.

4. ______

5. ______

6. ______

7. ______

8. ______

9. ______

Look at these prefixes: *de, ex, im, pro, sup,* and *trans.* They appear on many words, so they are good for mix-matching. Try to mix-match two of them with two different endings. Write the four words you made.

______

______

3. Animal Metaphors

Many common metaphors compare people with birds, animals, and other creatures. A person who likes staying up late is a "night owl." A person who pretends to be something he or she is not is sometimes called a "wolf in sheep's clothing."

To complete each of the metaphors below, write in the name of one of these creatures.

beaver	butterfly	duck	fox	puss
bird	cat	elephant	hog	worm

1. A very fearful person is a scaredy ______________________.
2. A person who likes to get up at dawn is an early ______________________.
3. A student who works hard is an eager ______________________.
4. A useless, but expensive, gift is a white ______________________.
5. A person who seldom smiles is a sour ______________________.
6. A student who loves to read is a book ______________________.
7. A driver who straddles two lanes is a road ______________________.
8. A person who gets away with playing tricks on others is a sly ______________________.
9. A mayor who can't run for another term is a lame ______________________.
10. A person who flits from one party to another is a social ______________________.

4. Coloring the Meaning

"He was born with a *silver* spoon in his mouth" means "His parents are rich."

"She sees the world through *rose*-colored glasses" means "She has a happy outlook."

Our language uses colors to express many meanings. Match each *color-full* sentence in column one with its meaning in column two. Write the letter of the matching meaning on each line.

Column 1		Column 2
1. ______	I'm singing the *blues*.	A. I'm jealous.
2. ______	I'm in the *pink* of condition.	B. I'm sad.
3. ______	I'm *green* with envy.	C. I'm healthy.
4. ______	It was *yellow* of me to run away.	D. I had a special occasion.
5. ______	It was a *red*-letter day for me.	E. I was cowardly.

The vocabulary of color goes far beyond those colors mentioned above. There are hues, or gradations, of each color. Match the color in column one with its hue in column two.

Column 1		Column 2
1. ______	brown	A. navy
2. ______	red	B. tan
3. ______	purple	C. emerald
4. ______	blue	D. scarlet
5. ______	green	E. mauve

5. Clipping Words

You know that *lab* is short for *laboratory* and *plane* is short for *airplane*. These words have been shortened or clipped by common use. Do you know the shorter word that can be made by clipping each of the longer words below? If so, write it on the line.

1. gymnasium ______________________
2. champion ______________________
3. examination ______________________
4. mathematics ______________________
5. referee ______________________
6. influenza ______________________
7. tuxedo ______________________
8. dormitory ______________________
9. microphone ______________________
10. veterinarian ______________________

6. Riddle Pairs

The following pairs of words sound alike, but have different spellings and meanings. Use these adjective-noun pairs to answer the first five riddles below.

bare	bear
hoarse	horse
dear	deer
cellar	seller
stationary	stationery

1. What do you call a lovable forest animal? __________
2. What is an undressed grizzly? __________
3. What do you call notepaper that does not move? __________
4. What is a pony with a sore throat? __________
5. What is a salesperson in a basement store? __________

Use these noun-verb sentences to write the rest of the answers.

Paws pause.
Eight ate.
Blue blew.
They're there.
We'd weed.

6. How many people finished dinner? __________
7. What color sounded the whistle? __________
8. Where are they? __________
9. What would we do if dandelions sprouted up all over the yard? __________
10. What happens when cats stop scratching? __________